DEEPLY SLEEPLESS

75 Collected Poems About Love, Death, & Everything

Beverly Van Pelt

BALBOA.PRESS
A DIVISION OF HAY HOUSE

Copyright © 2020 Beverly Van Pelt.

All rights reserved. No part of this book may be used or reproduced by any means, graphic, electronic, or mechanical, including photocopying, recording, taping or by any information storage retrieval system without the written permission of the author except in the case of brief quotations embodied in critical articles and reviews.

Balboa Press books may be ordered through booksellers or by contacting:

Balboa Press
A Division of Hay House
1663 Liberty Drive
Bloomington, IN 47403
www.balboapress.com
844-682-1282

Because of the dynamic nature of the Internet, any web addresses or links contained in this book may have changed since publication and may no longer be valid. The views expressed in this work are solely those of the author and do not necessarily reflect the views of the publisher, and the publisher hereby disclaims any responsibility for them.

This is a work of fiction. All of the characters, names, incidents, organizations, and dialogue in this novel are either the products of the author's imagination or are used fictitiously.

Cover art and Illustrations by Beverly Van Pelt

Print information available on the last page.

ISBN: 978-1-9822-5875-7 (sc)
ISBN: 978-1-9822-5877-1 (hc)
ISBN: 978-1-9822-5876-4 (e)

Library of Congress Control Number: 2020922878

Balboa Press rev. date: 11/27/2020

POE
TRY

Contents

Dedication ... ix
Foreword ... xi
Preface ... xiii

sleep ... 1
angst ... 11
love ... 21
breath ... 37
death ... 53
story ... 61
awake in bed ... 79
boundaries ... 89
time & seasons ... 103

Dedication

To the men in my life:

My father, Philip, who never had the opportunity to read my work. I love and miss you every day!

My son, Dane, who will have every opportunity to read my work. You are the greatest blessing I have ever been graced with, and you give me a joy that transcends my life. Never lose sight of your poetry, stories, and music for the world needs the power of your Spirit. I love you, my son!

To my husband, Patrick, who has read all of this work, over and over, and still wanted me to publish it. You are my muse. You are the reason my heart leaps. You cause me insomnia, and soothe me to sleep. You wake me with coffee and force me to eat. Even with all the words I write, you will never fully know how grateful I am that you have unlocked the secret chamber in my heart, liberating this free spirit to once again love, and create, and live.

Foreword

My most vivid memory of you, Beverly, was your spirited dancing one foggy September night on the California coast.

The Big Sur Fashion Show was celebrating its success with a grand finale that acknowledged the best of Big Sur—unconventional freedoms, creative artistry, and community spirit. Everyone had come together in one exuberant dance of joy.

Your hair shone blue in the misty light as we paid tribute to couture made of shells, feathers, chicken feed bags, coffee filters, and waffles . . . and as we honored the rugged resilience of friends and neighbors who have had to survive wildfires, landslides, stormy seas, earthquakes, floods, and droughts delivered with unfair persistence.

This moment reflected your power as a creative director, designer, actor, model, and charismatic figure in the community.

But there is always more to know.

With this book of poems, you unveil deeper layers, as yet unseen by all but your most intimate soulmates. Such revelations take courage. The poetic seeds were sown in you long ago. Now, they thrive. The time is right . . . for deliverance.

We meet the insomniac, the sufferer, the questioner, the truth teller, the restless soul, the enlightened mind, and, above all, the lover.

We also meet the data asset manager, who has tried to bring structure to these layers of life— from death and angst to sleep and breath. But, at the end of the day (or was it at the edges of night?), you no doubt realized, as we do after reading your work, that you cannot hide the all-too-obvious underlying theme—love.

This feeling woven throughout the book comes at a particularly welcome time, when internet doomscrolling is all too common and many of us in the world feel alone. The sheer power of your love extends beyond the pages of this book.

You introduce us to the lone angel, who "would rather whisper the truth to shatter the walls than to be the downfall of men." You admit that "the heart desires purity in purpose . . . nothing more." You know that "it will never be the same day—day after day. And that each day comes with a choice." You have given us important clues as to "what makes us human in this inhuman world." You give us a reason to choose life.

Poetry focuses on emotions and feelings. Stories are told sparingly. The words must be carefully chosen, because each has power.

Your words reflect this precision. They flow like the music that you so admire in your partner and muse—"earthbound and heavenly" at the same time.

The moments shared here—both monumental and mundane—all lead to your final conclusion.

"We may not save the world, but if we save each other, then it all seems worthwhile."

Well done. But let us not underestimate the power of poetry.

The world, too, can be saved. Thank you for this feeling of hope.

Meredith Mullins Paris, France
Author of the award-winning book, "In a Paris Moment"
Writer/ Fine Art Photographer for OIC Moments, Bonjour Paris, Paris Magazine, and National Geographic School Publishing
www.meredithmullins.artspan.com

Preface

My father died.

Sometimes it takes an event like that to bring everything into perspective.

I've been writing poetry for 37 years, a little longer if you count high school, which I usually don't. My true poetic life began in my first semester at college (1984) when I took a lower division Poetry class. For three hours every week, we had dedicated class time to analyze our feelings and to write poetry. This was when I started to recognize my influences, namely New Wave music, and fell in love with my favorite poets: Emily Dickinson, Edgar Allan Poe, Henry Wadsworth Longfellow, and e.e. cummings.

My poems became a type of signature for me. Having learned the structures and restrictions of poetry, I quickly began to break the rules, developing and delivering my own voice. My work had been presented on AM Radio Shows when I was a Guest, printed in various college newspapers, exhibited in visual artwork, incorporated into songs and videos, posted on websites and social media, but never published in a book. I AM a Poet. Performing in alternative forms is my thing, yesteryear and today!

And then my father died.

Suddenly I stepped back to do the proverbial "survey of my life". If I died tomorrow, what would happen? Would anyone know what I wanted for my coffin? Would anyone remember any of the ephemeral and esoteric places where I had presented my work? Would anyone understand my poetry in a way to publish it posthumously?

I thought back. What would my dad do if he were me?

I never shared my poetry with him, but he knew I was writing. We rarely discussed the topic, then, one day twenty years ago, he gave me a copy of a book of poetry written by my great-grandmother and two great-aunts. At the time, he suggested that I might consider doing something like that too. But I never did. Still, he had handed me my answer in the form of a book.

My dad always knew what to do. It only took twenty years for his message to go from his voice to my brain. Sometimes you just hear the message when it's the right time.

About this Book

When I made the commitment to publish my work, I was faced with a series of daunting tasks: search through thousands of pieces of paper, email, and social media posts to find my poetry – sorting into categories of poetry, poetic prose, short stories; wrangle some control over my work by organizing it into a workable format; choose the theme and select the best poems to fit it, then going back to change the theme – rinse and repeat. As a creative person, I hit the biggest roadblock of all: logistics. After agonizing over making no progress, the answer came to me in the most ironic of ways. I have worked in digital asset management (DAM). Could I possibly use logic and science to wrestle all of the words and feelings into a spreadsheet? The answer was YES!

Taking years of emotional outpouring, I was able to unemotionally get it into a MS Excel spreadsheet where it could live together in a safe community of verse. And that's when I realized that I had dated virtually every poem I had ever written. That seemed like an interesting piece of data so I added a column for that. Then I was curious about the word counts – added that to a column. Keywords – added to a column. Once I entered everything I had found up to that date, I was astonished at the volume.

I copied verses I wanted to use into a MS Word document, and sorted the Excel sheet by date. This presented a new problem. With so many entries, it was really hard to match up between the two types of documents.

You will notice as you read this book, that each poem has a number. Don't mistake this for the title. It's another DAM process: assign each entry with a unique identifier… a number! To be sure, this numerical system doesn't relate to dates, names, moods, keywords, or anything else other than the order in which pieces were entered into my data sheet.

There is an order within each section, and an ebb and flow between the sections.

Sometimes two poems will share a word or one mood will flow into the next. This was a happy surprise for me as it seemed to really add to the cadence of the work as a whole.

This book is divided into sections: Sleep, Angst, Love, Breath, Death, Story, Awake in Bed, Boundaries, and finally, Time & Seasons. These headings developed organically as I started grouping printed pieces by theme.

I have suffered with insomnia for most of my life, often joking about my very serious fears of "missing out on something" and "not waking up in the morning". During these late nights and early mornings culminating at the dead hour of 3am, I get the urge to purge my feelings and quite often my work turns to the theme of Sleep… and more appropriately Sleeplessness. The struggle between these opposites - these reluctant lovers - is related to the next section, Angst.

Not usually coming from the "pit of despair", for me, Angst becomes a topic of poetic exorcism as I will work through anxiety and, to a certain degree, rage. Some of these come from an almost dispassionate resignation while others express more heat. It is the incidental presence of passion that connects Angst to Love.

In this section, Love begins with Angst. "Yesterday - I was alone." And as one reads, there is still the tone of resignation, even as it concludes in love. Not only does this echo back to the previous section, but it opens the door to the varied experiences of love including worship of my lover, surrender, and humor. Up until this point, there have only been references to my lover but here is where my muse lives. He is my heart. He is my Soul. He is my breath.

This heady feeling prevails in the next section, called Breath, and appropriately opens with:

> What wonder, contained,
> while the day does break.
> The moment monumental,
> in the encapsulated breath.

The feelings of love as breath dominate this particular portion of the book, though there are some references to suffocation. Loss of breath was inspired, in part, by the chronic sinus issues I have lived with, and on an unconscious level, I must have been feeling the ever-present air of my father's years-long battle with emphysema and lung cancer. This section aptly ends with:

> What joy have we in these moments brief,
> bring breath to my aspiration.
> Joy, yes, in my last breath.
> I touch your face and die in deep adoration.

Each line of this quatrain has a direct reference to dying and leads to directly into the section named Death. Originally, this was at the end of the book, symbolizing the end as well as being the end, but once I established the order of poems in Breath, it immediately became clear to me that these two sections were closely related.

This is the shortest section of the book and there is an abiding irony to that. The vast majority of my work is focused on Love and Death and the emotions surrounding these, but in terms of this collection, I trusted my intuition and chose only the pieces that really fit together. The final poem here names "the Scottish play" and bids you welcome to Stories.

Stories may be my favorite part of the book. I am, after all, a storyteller and there is something so joyous to me about these narrative poems, many of which dip into whimsy. Some are dreams; some are humorous; all make me smile.

The smiling continues into Awake in Bed. At first, most (maybe all) of these selections were in Love. And they do make sense there in terms of theme, but that section became huge and unruly. I laid out printed pages and decided to see if there was a natural break within the theme. As it happened, there was a clear definition between the state of being in Love and the act of being Awake in Bed. The last selection ends with the serious "and today I choose to stay," leading us into the ever-revelatory Boundaries.

Fittingly, the opening line of the opening poem states, "Oh, Boundaries!" I won't lie. These poems explore working within boundaries and also crossing them. As well, they contain more evocative language then the other sections. Admittedly, I need to continue my self-exploration in this area.

The transition into the final Time & Seasons begins with a heightened sense from "The beating speeds; / it never stops."; then moves us along to references about length of time, day of the week, and seasons of the year. At first I called this section Events and put all of the "birthday poetry" there. After working and arranging all of the other Headings and roughing out an order within each, it became clear that this was much more about the small and large passages of time. At the end of time, it's not the whole big world but the small intimate one that matters most.

We may not save the world
but if we save each other
than it all seems worthwhile.

Taking a step back to really look at this completed work, I can see that a new story has developed. Each poem is its own, separate, isolated tale and can stand alone from every other piece, but together, they reveal a world where sleeplessness gives way to emotion, love, humor, and sheds an honest and hopeful light on feelings like angst and pain.

This book has changed me forever. I hope it will change you too.

There is a music in my mind
that pushes me to rhyme.
It happens when I'm walking.
It leads me by the hand.

It haunts me.
It keeps me from my Sleep.
It drives me.
It helps me understand.

sleep

49

I hear an echo clamoring
in my bed chamber.
It tolls for me, beckoning
with expectant clarity.
To answer it,
to push open that door,
to lay down in slumber -
resting on the edge of night -
seems daunting. And yet it calls me
to close my eyes, threatens me
with sweet dreams, and I
cannot fight this strong urge
to recline.
Good night!

April 2, 2013

7

I wonder where wild turkeys sleep.
Is it on fences or in chaparral
or nestled quietly in the trees?
Do they perch on edges of cliff-steeps,
ready to launch if predators are near?
Perhaps they don't sleep at all,
standing tall having slept by day.
Nay, they could half-sleep anywhere,
having one of their kind as sentinel.
Where do the wild turkeys sleep?
Oh, how I long to peep
at these kingly creatures,
with their varied alluring features,
and know their mystery of sleep.

March 29, 2017

154

Sweet, princely man
forever bitten with the sleep.
Know you the life you live
is music on the sheets?
And yet the Bard is in you,
thousands of words to say.
So sleep now and rest
your weary voice and head
for in a moment I will join you
fast asleep in bed.

September 3, 2014

169

Exhausted!
Denying defeat.
Need rest.
Conquer in the morning.
Or afternoon.
Ask for help?
Who helps find sleep?
Morpheus may find me.

August 4, 2014

146

O, Glorious Moon in the sky,
peering down on me.
Know how much your truth belies
the sleep evading me.
And so I pour another glass of wine.
I open my squinty, cat-lined eyes
and move to recline
in my chamber festooned with candles
and consummated in companionship.

September 25, 2010

166

Once again, the clock's will is to strike at three
While my lover's drowsy speech beckons me
To the silent bedchamber
To the darkened room
To the ruby sheets of purgatory
And I will find my perfect place, next to him -
Next in line to fade into dreamlike ecstasy -
To fall even more deeply -
To sleep.

July 21, 2013

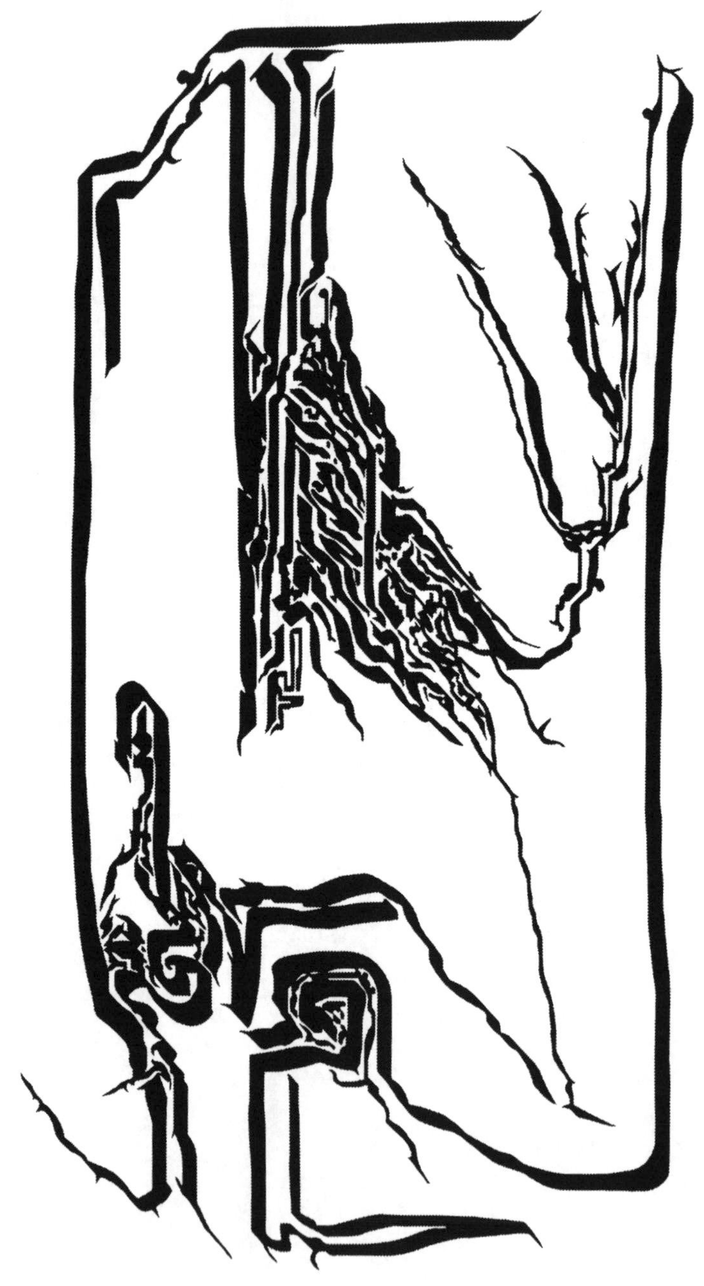

angst

33

The night calls my name,
calls from far, far away.
Calls me into clear skies
where dreams and hopes
go to die.
The Killing Moon
watches over fallen angels,
cheerful sprites,
guitar virtuosi,
the broken poetess-
beckoning truth
from bruised lips
and harmonies of the mind;
the very last thought.
O, Shakespeare,
where would this tale end?
There is but one state,
that of being,
in which all creatures
rise or fall-
that of grace.

February 23, 2015

37

There. In that tree.
A bird sings of sorrow.
Sweet. Sad. Sorrow.
And I cannot defend
against its affect.
I give in. Slowly at first
but soon am
abandoned to it.
I sob.
Why?
Why so sad
when it's only nature
and nature's cruel reality?
I sob until I'm sick.
It's the nausea
of the visceral knowledge.
That which needs
not be spoken
but is felt in all
of one's cells.
It is the sad.
It is the sad
of the Universe.
The birds in the trees
sing of it
and only a few
will hear.

June 22, 2014

110

I am a malcontent.
My mind is overactive
when my body begs for rest.
My brain explodes.
"More! I need more!"
"In what direction do I go?"
"Why? Why? Why?"
And the more I ask,
the more tired my sack of bones becomes.
I am a restless Soul-
not able to live
in a body
or in a mind.

May 7, 1987

56

WITH TRAGIC CONSEQUENCE I HOLD MY FISTS AWAY

With tragic consequence I hold my fists away.
One day, one night, one crowded space -
the wall that came between us -
nothing in collapse, only slow decay.
I think a dirty street would be a safer place.

And there the lights of burned out sky
take aim with deadly care.
Another place, another name -
would only break the glass of time
trapping us together in constant rage.

April 30, 2010

160

There is, by what is right
in a mind of wrong,
an appetite.
There - is where
the mind matters most
and is left to its own devices
in a sea of choices ill-gotten.
You see, it is a song
expressed on cold lips
for dead feelings -
catering to despair,
and tequila sips in rusty cups,
but never conceived of
as just another excuse
binding the past
to the unclean Soul.
This appetite for chaos
hides a forbidden truth –
that the heart desires
purity in purpose.
Nothing more.

September 1, 2019

94

I see you crying, lying next to me –
opening your arms, holding me.
In the desert we found our fate.
Do you remember China Lake?
And together we made our way
wandering out in the wild rain.
Water shimmering upon our skin –
climbing upward - climbing in.
And we wondered if it could last –
now all we've got left is the past.

Your tears fall. They shower me –
holding my arms, holding me.
You said you'd love me forever a day.
Do you remember the promise I made?
Together and together and together that way
never questioning . . .

July 27, 1999

love

43

Yesterday - I was alone.
I sat in diffused light
out of sight
of tv's, kitchens, and phones.
A thought I captured.
It poured salt on my head.
And instead of pain,
I was enraptured.
Crystallized in time,
there is but one dream.
It would seem
Love is destined to be mine.

January 19, 2014

35

I wonder at your gigantic brain
and marvel at your lovely feet.
(What! I do! And that's the truth!)
Somewhere in the subterrane
is the memory of our first retreat
from a world of monstrous vain
and shallow, fallow conceit.
Then, and only then, when the sun
threatens to breach our exposed
purpose, we collapse in a heap
of honest flesh and love-soaked,
heaven-sent adoration between
you and me and our Valentine's prize,
be it here or there or fast asleep
in each other's long embrace.
There, we will find an ecstatic
foray to our time-piece Soul,
also known as our united heart,
where we linger and linger
and love and love
and force out the ill fates
of the monstrously vain *speck*

so that artistic fires in our minds
will have space to find
the open stage and perform
until our guts are spilled
on the field of battle,
by which I mean to say,
We put on stage our blazing
Passion for the Work.
To this I vow, and to you,
A Valentine's was never as true
as the one we are making today.

February 13, 2015

32

Live. Love. Laugh. Die.
It's so much work.
So much.
We cry. We kiss. We try. We miss.
Sometimes.
Sometimes.
A day breaks. The dead awake.
Some start believing.
Some do.
Fate. Up against the Will.
Some surrender.
Some never will.
I yielded.
I died.
I opened my Soul.
You surrendered.
You lived.
You revealed your Heart.
And now, we two,
have one Heart -
have one Soul.

February 23, 2015

13

O, joy!
He hath the heart to comfort me,
to hold me in his eye.
He cradles me in his sultry lips
that taste of whiskey rye.
And when he says he loves me,
he says it while he cries.
He says he'll love me all his life
even when he's dry.

October 19, 2016

19

Were I to love you less,
I would be unfulfilled.
But to love you more
is a future I've yet to build.
For love increases every day
and is the life I wish today.

You may think this is just about you,
but that would be a mistake.
For it is as much about our child
and the happiness he makes.

September 23, 2016

5

I watch your Kleos glow
in golden waves of glory –
serving the muse with honorarium-
serving the goddess of sound-
earning your own timé
in your own time –
in your own way.
I would have it not as any other
for your tall shadow
cools the heat of battle
and heats me to my core.
You sing songs of all else
but love pours from your lips
in the silence between the strings.

Thank you, my dearest Love.
My heart.
My muse.

April 18, 2018

152

What rapturous bliss,
I tell you, exists
within the heavenly
and well perfumed kiss
of the encounter
under a new moon
when doubt no longer insists
and you know the truth.

August 21, 2009

55

Love is an irrepressible thing
made up of perfume
and the honeybee's sting.
But when there's room
in the heart to sing,
Love shall bloom
near the end of Spring.

May 22, 2010

162

O, how you make life feel worthwhile,
as you love one such as I.
May tomorrow be of the stuff such as this,
that one may love such as I.

June 1, 2015

99

Were there but you and I
alone in this dire world -
You, lightest beauty and mind -
I, in your radiance, engaged -
each day, each moment,
each grain of sand
would wash over time fleeting -
I would worship through our embrace
and live a lifetime
in each moist breath.

There is but you and I
alone amid a forest of Ghosts -
You, golden Oak, a Spire -
I, in vapor form, entwined -
the grave whisper of moss,
entanglement of shade -
I dive deep to worship your roots.
My lips search your Kiss
in the damp fog.

Wherefore you and I
Alone amid a populace of Souls -
You.
I.

July 26, 1999

61

What precious (oh, my Precious!)
What precious man are you
that cometh with sweet words
of love and thank you?
Have you not the same sense as I,
that though I choose you,
we've lived this life?
The choose is universal and divine –
that two shall meet at that first moment in time
and forever then all their lives are entwined.
So there it is. I choose this entwined form.
Your legs and arms,
your steely mind and artful charms
are sweet intoxication –
like eggnog or mince pie –
and my blackened heart, now in the light,
will never die alone.

So thank you, my Precious man.
Thank you, my sweet dessert.
Thank you, my medieval wine
of pomegranate and sour apple
that has set upon to bloom in enchanted aroma.
Thank you, my pet for granting me
our Christmas custom and child-like reveries.

November 29, 2004

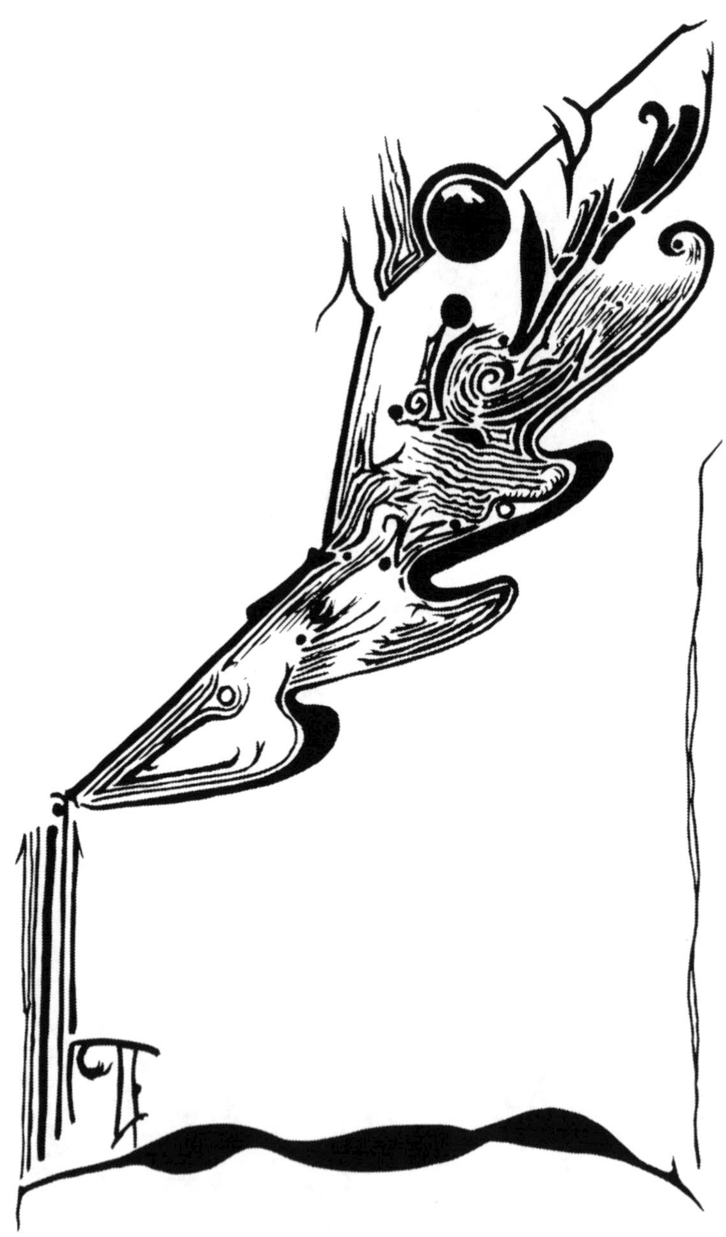

breath

3

What wonder, contained,
while the day does break.
The moment monumental,
in the encapsulated breath.
Yet, as I reel through memories-
as I scale past thought-
I release all feeling, free to float
on theories of string
and elaborate astral colors
that drift unencumbered
through stardust and sleep.
Uplifted and gravity-free,
that is to say, without grave thought
or thoughts of the grave,
I levitate in grey space,
while pyramidal powers
rejuvenate a lust for life.
To breathe. Perchance to see.
Living is more than feeling.
It is in living that we learn to be.

July 2, 2019

105

WHEN LAST NIGHT YOU…

When last night you whispered in my ear,
your breath entered me
sending a shiver that ignited the very muscles
that keep the imagination alive –
When last night you whisked the hair
off of one shoulder, over my neck,
your finger brushing my skin
leaving a warm trail of arousal –
When last night you moved your body
lifting me to your place and down
living there for hours
until we two were blended –

Now the ache remains.
Consumed by desire
with thoughts of our sauna-like bed.
Steam burning and dripping.
Your wet hair dripping on me.
Your strong approach and gentle guidance.
Your strong release and tears of joy.
Remaining, holding of each other.
When last night you called my name
from slumbering after-memories
and moaned in deep satisfaction,
my body responded in kind.

February 14, 2005

40

There's a place within the space of time
where I relive certain, perfect moments;
when you looked deeply into my eyes
and drew out my timid, angry Soul,
coaxing the light from near complete darkness;
when there was the bunny-kitty talk
and the next day a wild rabbit magically appeared;
when I was dying and you stayed with me
(giving me the strength to tell jokes to the doctors!)
and wouldn't let me drift away with the beckoning light;
when I saw you hold our son and you glowed-
emanating your namely luster, as did our beloved boy;
when the montage rolls - your triumphs on stage
starting with Hedwig, running through Flamenco,
banging the metal, composing music that
makes my whole world make sense somehow;
when you walked up to me with a big, mustachioed grin
and handed me the perfect Bloody Mary
because you knew my bad day would be cheered;
when I heard your voice, your somber, low rumble
that took my breath away and still makes me tremble.
I used to live there, lingering in sweet memory.
I forgot how to live.

You forgot how to live.
And then, through Alchemy, you reached out anew,
with violent breath and a passion for life.
I said to you:
"O, husband, there are so many of those old moments
that I feel frozen in time -
here in this place within the space of time."
And you responded
with a time-shattering kiss.

May 5, 2014

26

How soft you breathe in your deepest sleep -
like a whisper,
like a far away dream.
Much sooner do you wake upon your pillow -
stretching, bending back, your face aglow.
It is your beard that stays awake -
for its own sake -
and waves to me as if my hand to shake.
But it is your brain that I long to know -
for where IT is, the rest of you will go.

August 5, 2015

108

Tomorrow – Good Morrow –
darkness has veiled my eyes
and I see nothing.

Now the dungeon's stench
swells in my lungs –
shall the Sun streak the Heavens again?

My Night has fallen –
betrayed by the Sun of a passing day.
He is dead now.

I shiver here,
believing he will rise one day
to extinguish the torch
of the Killing Sun.

The Moon Warrior
also betrays me
with his false promise to return.

Now the dungeon's stench
steals my last breath.

August 9, 1986

122

Alone
we sit here
in the dark-
in the quiet.
Your hand touches mine
and I fear you cannot see.
Slowly, you lean over-
you kiss me.
Perhaps it is I who am blind
with tears filling my eyes.
It's been so long.
You lay your hand on my bare thigh
and I close my eyes.
Softly, you kiss me again.
This time you break the silence
with a mere whisper.
"What are you thinking of?"
You move your hand-
it warms my sensitive skin.
Breathlessly I say, in barely a voice,
"Your hand… Your lips…"
You are stealing my last breath
as you lightly brush my neck.

January 1, 1985

140

Love #5

The vein moves –
cadence is strong
Smooth and regular
Calm.
Skin surround –
tranquil
serene
cool and even.
White blonde hair –
trails gently
cut close
glows softly.
Down –
muscles curve
shoulders, strong
descendingly cove.
Slightest movement –
fixed, quiet
Breath
misty whisper.
My lips part.
I start toward you,
respondingly greeted
by your back.

October 30, 1998

118

Early in the morning,
after a restless night's sleep,
I turn to the open window.
The air "feels" cool and fresh,
but the moisture is heavy in my lungs.
And as my eyes focus,
there is grey,
for behind a thick wall of fog,
I sense a freed sun.
How dim this world seems.

Were the fog not here,
light would expose all things,
and the Earth would be allowed
to present itself to me-
a mere human.

But for now,
the greedy fog hangs,
in its unthinking, unfeeling way,
obscuring from sight
what is REALITY.

March 27, 1985

133

My Soul is chained to a crippled tree
mulched in between forest leaves –
longing to linger, singer of songs –
cuffed and clasping, repenting my wrongs.

Shackle me! Shackled – never free.
Asphyxia in the cool, clean breeze.
Land falls heavy, lands on my head –
my heart stands ready – ready, set, Dead.

Foreordained by forged-iron chain –
leashed to the spike of this mortal strain.

… because here he comes…

Chain, iron, restraint, shackle, leash, tie

April 18, 1997

137

MORE ALLEGORY
Opus No. 1

HOMAGE TO 'DECLENSION'

Which tree
stands across the street –
swaying slowly
to the meter
measured in noise
and stretched
skyward to escape
the encroaching traffic –
people pollution
(corruption of the Soul) –
straining to maintain
some sort of noble
refrain untainted?
Only one –
tall, crippling extension –
some similar cancerous growth –
popping its Earthly skin
plunging desperately

into the upper ether,
gasping for clean air,
searching for purity
while destroying
the building's Foundation
with deep, ancient
tendril roots –
having survived
nutrient poverty.

Decay of space
contained within crumbled walls;
decay of bones –
dirt floor is warm and dry;
one glance shows sky
through the vine-opened roof;
simplicity is grey and beige.
Lying on the cold Stone,
one knows
Devotion is hard on the Eye.

November 3, 1998

149

What joy have we in these moments brief,
bring breath to my aspiration.
Joy, yes, in my last breath.
I touch your face and die in deep adoration.

July 30, 2012

death

20

One day, one way
to love a castaway.
You were left out.
Cast-about
with one card left to play.
You turned it over
and found me there,
hiding in a bar.
There we hid,
Covered in gin,
drinking from a jar.
Then I looked up --
and saw you spread your wings.
How radiant! How gold!
How much happiness you bring!
That's how we began to unfold.
You, an angel, floating on air.
Me, a mortal, accepting a dare.
Here we are, 20 years hence,
holding off Death and taxes.
And so I must ask,
"Shall we dance(?)
'til death do part us
and we are covered in dust?"

September 21, 2016

54

What towering Angel roams
and finds us in our plight.
Serves an overview of what lies
beyond this domain.

What sight horrifies you?
What demon comes to mind?
What avenue to escape from?
Never mind. It's too late for you.

What light shines over you?
What lies beyond your time?
Beyond this place of being
finds your lost ghostly coil.

And dying with you in my arms –
Escape this tragic plague
to rise up and destroy them

May 23, 2010

93

WEAR BLACK

Morbidity is mine says the girl made of sunshine!
So then, lover,
I hope you don't mind
being the recipient
of all my angst.

When I die,
I want you to wear black.
Not just your tie or your slacks
But everything.
Wear a black suit and hat -
And why don't you wear a black shirt with that.

I know you'll complain that you've nothing to wear.
"The dry cleaner has all of my blacks
so why don't I just dress in grey?"
And you'll listen for what I'll say
as though I'll speak to you from the grave.

Is it all too much to ask?
It'll be the last time I give you a task.
So start looking now on every sales rack
'cause when I die,
I want you to wear black.

July 30, 1999

38

Mind is overwhelmed by emotion.
Emotions have all been bled.
Keep the body in motion;
I can sleep when I am dead.

June 2, 2014

167

Blue of nature
shown in red light -
his eyes were violet,
intense, filled with fright.
The specter was real
at least to Macbeth
who followed it into
the eye of Death.

July 19, 2013

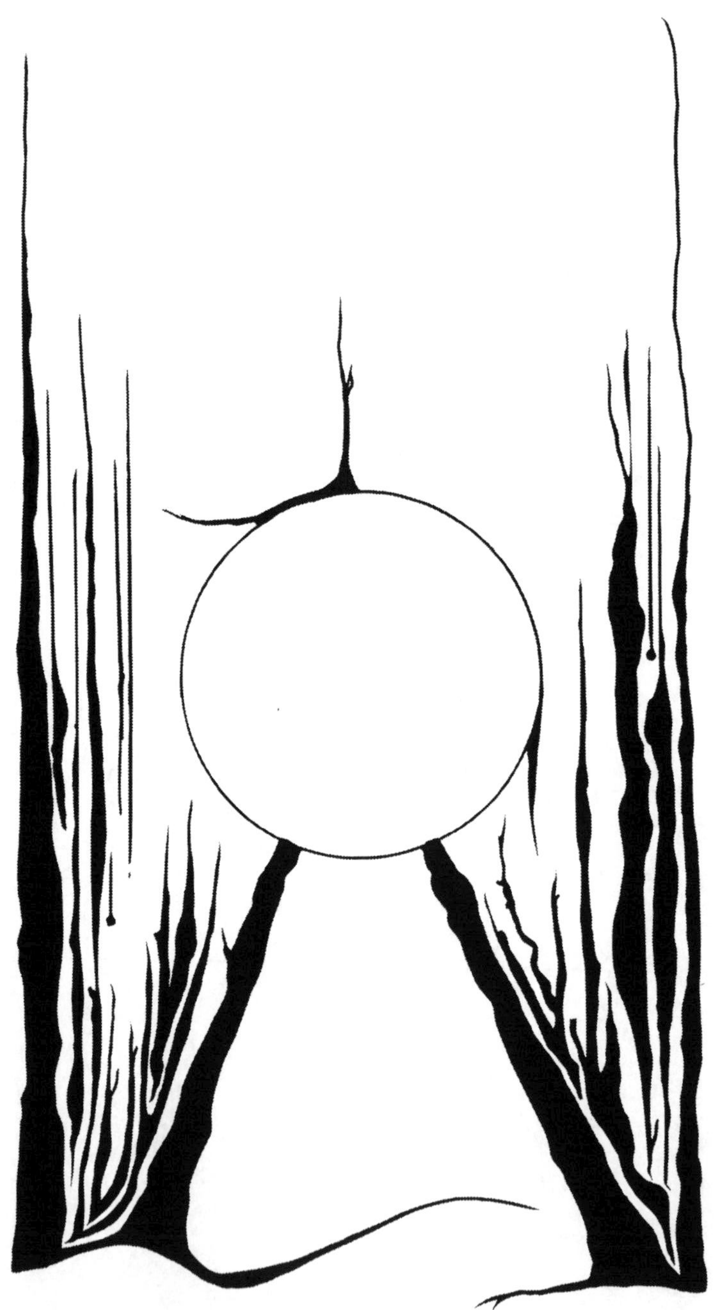

story

6

WERE I CAT WOMAN

Were I Cat Woman,
I would jump on a fence-
I would climb a tree-
I would chase after butterflies and scratch at bees.
I would bathe for hours
while planning to nap.
I'd bat around tinsel
and eat tuna for lunch.
When the sun would finally drift
into my South facing window,
I'd circle around
and stretch out
on my stolen Persian rug,
there napping again,
with dreams of diamonds...
and throwing knives.
Happily waking
to the Robin's song,
my next caper would be afoot.

I would run and jump and climb,
making my dangerous way
to the sounds of the City.
IF... IF I were to get caught,
surely Gotham's Force
would needs ask,
"What was your motivation?"
I would think to myself,
"To find Joy in the pursuit,
using my intelligence
for material gain,
even while climbing
on the backs of men."
But I wouldn't say that.
Oh no! I would not.
Instead,
with my feline smile,
I'd say,
"What else could it be?
I long to be with Batman
and he longs to be with me."

March 9, 2018

58

THE GARDEN GNOME

Wispy wind and whiskey breath,
the Gnome seems to like his new address.
Up the drive and to the right
is where you'll see him pick a fight.
Poor white cat has no chance
against his fist and sideways glance.
In the warm and balmy night,
mosquitoes won't get a single bite.
Frosty days and frozen nights,
good thing Gnome has on his tights.
And when the family goes out to play,
grumpy Gnome has nothing to say.

March 11, 2005

41

I have a troll
with two blue eyes
in one blue socket.
He's tall, not lanky.
His beard is full of beer.
His humor is droll and
he lives in my pocket...
but that's not why he's cranky!

April 24, 2014

42

O, glorious Beard!
Thou doth speak to me
as threads of spun Gold
upon a spinning wheel.
Yielding and unbreakable,
glinting in starlight,
silkened by Exotic Oils,
caressed by mine own
tiny fingers, twisting curls.
And then there was
the mustacchio.

April 2, 2014

18

Waking at early sunrise
on the cool sand of the beach,
I quiver and reach for my sweater.
The waves froth as they approach,
the salt-mist stings at my wind-burnt face.
Here at the edge of the world
it all feels fragile and yet new
like a fresh start or the end of life.
Why am I here? I can't remember.
In the quiet moments before
the gulls arrive to find a feast
left in the retreating tides,
I hear the thumping of my heart
and the breath strained
through my dry throat and pressed lung;
not labored, just noticed
in the silence of my thoughts.
How very alone this is.
That's the thought I have
when a swarm of gulls call out
their arrival and the golden hour
rises to the day.

Why am I here?
It isn't wrong to be here,
and it isn't right. It is, and it isn't.
As the sun crests over
my neighboring dune,
and the early morning walkers
start out on their search
for shells and washed up bodies,
I gather up my shoes, and keys,
and with a long last breath,
I give up asking why
and just try to remember:
where is my car?

September 27, 2016

159

'Twixt grey fog and nightfall
there dwells uncertain fate.
My ride careens
along the twisted highway.
Screeching brakes.
Accelerates.
The fog deepens
and fear creeps into mind.
Pull hard to the left.
Scream!
Oh. It's only a balloon.

August 24, 2009

29

For tonight the stars burn my eyes
and their flames sear my skin.
Thus began the dream I had
before the nightmare began.
The forest at night was foreboding
with fallen stars exploding
into nearby villages with thunderous
displays of destruction.
Water, all water, evaporated
into the clouds.
Into those chemical houses
of greedy politicians
and dwelling places for the evil ones.
Peaking through the small spaces,
between the fire and water,
I saw no movement - still air.
Far from the safest star,
between the rocks and graves
in the fallow fields
sat a lone angel,
fallen but not evil.
One who would rather whisper the truth
to shatter the walls,
than to be the downfall of men.

February 26, 2015

138

CAT-ER-COUS-IN

<Ring around the Pansies.
Dressing up all Fancy.
Ask us. Ask us.
We all go Crazy.>

Latin Katin gave the call
Reaching downward not to fall.
When the knife flew past her eye,
She found herself sliding by.

Driving whiplash, turn the key –
"Sometimes quiet's not for me."
Judgment hanging over head,
Wisdom stalling, never said.

One step forward, two steps back.
Feels like something – Soul attacked.
Reaching upward, falling down.
Easy answers never found.

Drink the tonic – catatonic –
Awaking at the End.
Tastes like Romance – acts dynamic –
Beginning once again.

August 28, 1998

134

OVERLAY IN GOLD
Opus. #2

She withstood
amidst the nest of coffins.
One sway left
another right,
a door slammed in a separate room;
She twitched involuntarily
- sighed a deep breath –
Her mild eyes followed the line
of sarcophagi.
Head down,
she accepted her strain
and moved onto the approach.
Softly, left hand to chest,
she caressed the front casket.
Gold gilded as it was,
she managed, with care,
to wipe away
the spots of now cold tears
with the white cloth
she pulled from her pocket.

Then her eyes fell
to the head-marker Gold-engraved,
"Poet, Humanitarian, Lover
'The Resurrected Soul'"
and, as the dim light filtered
through the stained glass
of the Funeral Home,
she saw multiple finger prints
obscuring the inscription.
She lifted the white cloth again,
cleaning with vigor –
erasing the violation of Sanctity;
her intent was aimed for perfection.

The door opened slowly –
it scraped grey carpet with its wood.
Fingers emerged –
wrapped the jamb.
Spreading into the light
was another woman.
"When you're finished here,
start cleaning the Sales Office."

November 4, 1998

36

I married a man who is made of glass.
His mind is sharp, his wit is fast.
But when it comes to feet and bones,
he Cracks and Breaks and always Moans.
So when your man is apt to break,
make him wear shoes for Heaven's sake!

August 20, 2014

150

It was a wondrous thing that happened that day –
A baby boy came out to play.
Shy and sweet and O, so fair,
he grew so tall without a care.
When the guitar he started to play,
he knew the beast he had to slay.
With sweeping gestures and purest heart,
with genius light… and a foolish start,
he laid waste -
all were slain.
He left them to their horrid fate –
Yet – the conquering man was sad and sate.
One day his rampage fell on a Soul
who had lived her life inside a hole.
His rage, his state, his lingering gaze,
his sullen heart found ruins to raze.
He played! She lived! They loved!
They conceived A Gift from High Above!
Then the dust – it fell up!
It landed in the woman's cup.
As she pressed her lips to taste
(Death's Wine)

to take her sleep for all of time,
he took it gently from her hand
and wouldn't let her drink the sand.
He took his strings of hardest steel
and set to change his songs' appeal.
With love singing out true and loud,
Angels wept from every cloud.
He played! She lived! They loved!
She played! He lived! They loved!

February 22, 2012

awake in bed

80

Around the time the Sun begins to rise,
in the night-burning rays of light,
with the first stirrings of our child
and the Kitty-creepings done for the night;
as you gently turn in our bridal bed,
breathing so faintly,
a slight move of your head,
I whisper, "What are you dreaming?"
You smile - and blush lightly red.

September 14, 2002

155

Am I in love with love?
Why, yes. Yes I am.
Do I love love more than you?
I see you don't understand.
I didn't love love
before I loved you.
I loved red roses,
French cuisine & caviar.
I loved California Champagne,
Sandman Comics & chocolate.
I loved my cat & making omelets.
But I never loved life
until I met you.
I never shared Shakespeare
until I knew you.
I never smiled to myself
until I met you.
I never loved the rain,
or the desert,
or hours & hours awake in bed
until I was with you.
Do you now see why
I'm in love with love?
I'm in love with love
because I'm in love with you.

September 6, 2015

148

Whisked away to bed to play,
the morning soon shall rise.
Night-time endures
what love implores
until the darkness dies.

August 17, 2010

21

"He who sleeps last,
sleeps least."
or so the Swabbies say.
Don't wake him,
or shake him,
or else you'll have to pay.
But I have found,
if you kiss him gently on the neck
while tugging on his beard,
he awakes fairly easily.
There's naught to be a-feared.
And so this sleepy seaman
is off to snore what he must reap.
Until I come a callin'
to rouse him from his sleep.

April 5, 2016

59

O, Lord, you are my muse!
Man of the house
who rules the roost.
You - who knew me,
who held no hope
but still loved me well -
have lifted my life
from sadness & strife
so that I may be
a true woman
with dignity
enraptured
and one Christmas wish:
to be with my lover
beneath crisp, cold,
white cotton sheets

December 6, 2004

47

Where to wander in the folds of the mind
when we sleep between the creases
of an old, broken bed.
One place, one ruin, one memory
stands in front, begins to fade
like sun-drenched mist
over the green-blue bay.
"Stay here," he says.
"Stay with me," he whispers.
"Open your eyes," comes a voice
that is not his, nor mine.
And on waking, I know.
It will never be the same day -
day after day.
Each day comes with daylight;
each morning comes with a choice,
and today I choose to stay.

September 24, 2013

boundaries

168

Oh, Boundaries!
How you do elude me at times,
and yet, you are still pursued.
The key is to boost
my drive to respect you,
and thus the worth is proved!

July 18, 2018

165

Beautiful creatures, severed from birth
delivered unto this plain, this tethered earth.
"Fear not!" they tell you, and push you away.
"Be free as the wind!" while hung on a chain.
Then it comes to you quite by accident.
"Be yourself. Be pure of heart."
That rings true but just at the start.
"Fly as high as you can but don't touch the sun."
"Control your wings and manage your run."
"Praise the Spirit, and know you are One."
"Face your faults, and admit when you're wrong."
And that's how it is when Beautiful creatures
find themselves tethered to invisible features.

August 30, 2016

25

Who was this me?
A girl, a woman, a ghost
with one thing in mind:
Happily ever after.
So to waken from my sleep,
from my stupor slumber,
was not the wake-up call I expected
but a connection to a wrong number.
And the number wasn't wrong.
It was a great awakening
that opened these
coin-covered eyes
and lighted a path
to the happiness
I had always wanted.
And knowing that Karma
happens regardless of me,
makes the not caring
even more sweet.
It will happen even
without my stead.

September 4, 2015

91

My Darling-

To whom would I confide
were you not in my life?
Perhaps only
to the wind or the sea,
the Universal Deity
or mine own feet -
only some zygote
of everything
would almost be enough
to approach
my confidence
(confidentially)
in you.

October 7, 1999

161

SOME TRASH SHOULDN'T BE RECYCLED

When about,
turn around.
Bend the other way.
When in doubt,
cast them out.
Toss the trash away!
When they're out,
do not doubt.
Keep the trash at bay.
While they're out,
on their route,
the trashmen taketh away.
When they're gone,
and all is done,
that trash will soon decay!

Some trash shouldn't be recycled.

June 25, 2017

139

Why do you arm mine enemies
with proofs against my security?
Were I not traveling away
from this stagnant place
(on the Eastern road
In Search Of the other path),
I would have cursed you –
wickedly,
viciously,
reflecting back to you
the pain of your betrayal –
and vindictively
stayed to watch
the disintegration of your Soul.

Ah, but, though I am flawed,
I seek a higher truth.

1984

23

There was a spectre that darkened my door.
That soiled the path I trod.
Truth was absent from his lips
long before his fraud.
And how I frowned and frowned,
drowned in mystery and fear.
How I lived I cannot say
but I nearly died each single day -
from threats, from lies, from that sadistic man.
From his drugs and alcoholic lifestyle.
The day after I left was the first I'd slept,
and woke up in the morn
with the revelation that from then on,
each sunrise was a new day born;
that each day built a new life.
I never once questioned that decision
and I know that's why today I'm alive!
That black spot of illness is dead.
Long live Life!

December 19, 2015

28

Oh Facebook!
Why art thou so stealthy
in thy caprice -
throwing malice
and malcontentment
in the unrested face
of one such as I?
Be aware and wary
of your intent
for in the World of Karma,
there is little room left
for those who step on others
and those who must resent.
And some people
lose automatically
because they're miserable examples
of what human beings should be.
Deserving no peace,
no sympathy, no attention,
no compassion, no relief.
So there you have it,
O' Book o' Face!
I release you for tonight.
Perhaps tomorrow
you will be less toxic -
more kind,
more gentle,
More... bucolic!

May 21, 2015

147

When the gothic architecture of my Soul lies in ruins -
when I walk on hands and knees across the thorns of sorrow -
when my tombstone is covered by the fallen leaves of decay -
my spirit will be obtainable.
Grasp at the wind and hold remembrance of me.
You will pull back the veil,
unleashing my prisoner-self as I rise
from my crypt and seek out your love.

September 21, 2010

157

Pools of cool water
sooth your dry skin
despite the arid day –
and wet your lips.
Revived, you move through
the sunlight hours,
not as a ghost (not like before)
but as a spirit –
free to move,
free to live,
free to be.
And when the hours
of darkness and winter come,
your Spirit will stay true,
warmed by simple embers
glowing like rubies in the Soul.

September 6, 2013

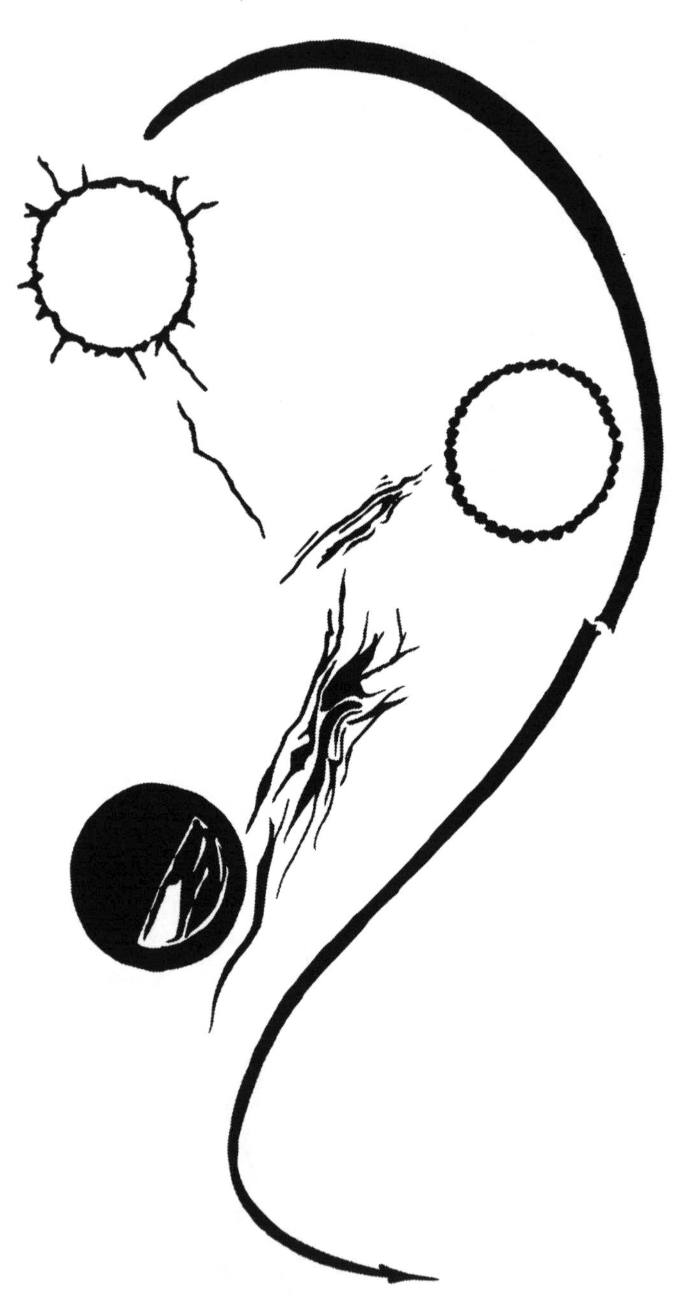

time & seasons

72

The beating speeds;
it never stops.
The heartache heels
when talking stops.

A long goodbye,
wrapped, your arms with mine,
with longing still –
our parting sigh.

Your strong embrace;
Your gentle kiss;
Your loving hand
is what I miss.

What joy I know
when home again.
It's the longest two hours
there's ever been.

July 30, 2003

15

Two in one -
The Spirit song -
Come play with us
this season long.
The Autumn leaves
and setting sun
will remind us now
the day is gone.
Two in one -
Come, oh Spirit -
Come play with us
this season long.
When comes the rain,
and when the snow,
then the people
will finally know.
Two in one -
Feasting Spirit -
Come play with us
this season long.

October 5, 2016

2

ON THE OCCASION OF YOUR BIRTHDAY

This day is lighted in my heart
as the sun filters through waves
of high clouds and fog.
It is the brightness of his Soul
that stirs me into a passion
of celebratory thoughts and actions.
Will he make a wish upon his candles
for another year enlivened
by the force of youth
that we produced
some eight and ten years hence?
Yes.
And will he make another wish
for a gathering of musicians
to perform his heart-songs
for those who adore them?
These are worthy of grace
and I pray they will come to pass.
And what of his sacred wish?
The one he keeps locked
in the secret chamber of his heart?

What of that?
What key is there to open that door
and cast a light on that deep desire?
I, too, have a profound wish
that I have locked securely in my heart,
protected from everyday maladies.
I love it and care for it,
unlocking that blood chamber
and bringing it into the light,
letting it breath and blossom,
outside of me
to shower upon him.
Yet, it is fragile, this embodied wish,
necessitating great care
and safe keeping. I hold the key.
Will this be the day, of the year,
of the lifetime, that we will
speak that which is securely held?
Maybe. Or perhaps our daily routines
act as the interpreters of these -
these most internal motives.
Let us then stand facing one another,
and simultaneously turning our keys,

open our secret gardens
to shine each light to the other
and know.
Until such, I have…
Faith without knowing.
Belief without seeing.
I feel it in my Soul.
You are an angel, trapped
in this mortal coil,
and making the most earth-bound
and heavenly music in the world.
You are my Valhalla.
You are my Glow.
You are my Precious.

February 23, 2020

10

I'll write you a threnody,
I'll sing you a song.
We're doubly blest,
you and I,
with a smart and handsome spawn.
Be elated from time to time
with your Golden Opportunities,
as your Romantic Soul demands,
and recognize the Jewels you hold
within your open hand.
We ARE gilded –
Solid, Plated, and Shiny –
watching that epic hour
as the sun sets gently
in our Color in the West
while we stand,
our feet in the soft white sand.

February 24, 2017

30

You were born at just the right time,
to be a joy, a boy, in the Pisces sign.
A few days earlier, you would been
a Rudolph or perhaps a Valentine.
A half year later you might have been
named for Elvis, the King.
A few minutes earlier or a few years off
and we would never, ever have met.
So I'm grateful for the Powers,
the Thrones and the Holies,
for blessing my life with you!
Happy birthday, my Love!

February 23, 2015

151

CHEERS for the Weekend, and
CHEERS for the beer!
Nothing screams Happy
like a glass of good cheer!

June 10, 2016

153

And Sunday is the day of freedom.
The day of sad remembrance
of the fun we recently had.
The Production is now over;
the cast has been dispersed.
All that's left is to toast
a brand new birth.
So with glad heart and mind to suit,
I break open this Champagne Brut!
Cheers to you, my Brave-at-Heart!
Congratulations are due.
I knew your talent from the start,
and now THEY know it too.

August 18, 2013

12

We may not be on stage together,
in May or ever,
but I've loved every moment
we've had there.
Perhaps I'm waxing poetic
on this, your birthday eve,
for reflection,
being a mirror,
recalls such moments
of understanding
that happen
only when two souls
choose to share a life
and experience tandem
Harmonies and Discords.
Do I regret ill words
between years of grace?
No. I can no more
unbelieve in those moments
than you can unstrum
your guitar or unspeak
your Shakespeare.
This makes me love you more.
It makes us human
in this inhuman world.
It makes us immortal
in this mortal coil.
It makes us grounded

in this in corporeal life.
Does my reflection
sound sad? I suppose so.
There IS something
sad within me.
And within you.
It is our Chiron karma,
our enduring bond
that, like pressure applied
from all sides,
locks us in ever
spiraling happiness
and sadness;
creativeness
and slumber.
Happy birthday, my love,
and happy years ahead.
We will drink champagne
and eat cake.
We will pet cats
and plant ideas.
We may not save the world
but if we save each other
than it all seems worthwhile.

February 23, 2017